First World War
and Army of Occupation
War Diary
France, Belgium and Germany

41 DIVISION
124 Infantry Brigade
Queen's (Royal West Surrey Regiment)
10th Battalion
1 March 1918 - 31 January 1919

WO95/2643/2

Published by

The Naval & Military Press Ltd

Unit 10 Ridgewood Industrial Park,

Uckfield, East Sussex,

TN22 5QE England

Tel: +44 (0) 1825 749494

www.naval-military-press.com

www.nmarchive.com

This diary has been reprinted in facsimile from the original. Any imperfections are inevitably reproduced and the quality may fall short of modern type and cartographic standards.

© **Crown Copyright**
Images reproduced by permission of The National Archives, London, England, 2015.

Contents

Document type	Place/Title	Date From	Date To
Heading	WO95/2643 (2)		
Heading	124th Inf. Bde. 41st Div. Battn. with Bde. re-Turned to France from Italy 1/6.3.18. War Diary 10th Battn. The Queen's Royal Regiment (West Surrey). March 1918.		
War Diary	Limena	01/03/1918	01/03/1918
War Diary	Suss St Leger.	05/03/1918	21/03/1918
War Diary	Bucquoy.	30/03/1918	31/03/1918
Heading	41st Division. 124th Infantry Brigade War Diary 10th Battalion The Royal West Surrey Regiment April 1918.		
War Diary	Bucquoy.	01/04/1918	08/04/1918
War Diary	Passchendale	13/04/1918	16/04/1918
War Diary	Ypres.	16/04/1918	31/05/1918
War Diary	Ypres Sheet 28 H.2.a.	01/06/1918	03/06/1918
War Diary	Hazebrouck 5a 1/40,000 Volkerinckhove	04/06/1918	08/06/1918
War Diary	Audrehem Sheet Calais 13.	10/06/1918	24/06/1918
War Diary	Audrehem Volkerinchove.	25/06/1918	26/06/1918
War Diary	Oudezeele.	27/06/1918	30/06/1918
War Diary	Sheet 27 1/40,000 W. Of Reninghelst.	30/06/1918	04/07/1918
War Diary	Sheet 28 Scherpenberg.	05/07/1918	14/07/1918
War Diary	Sheet 27. W. Of Reninghelst.	15/07/1918	15/07/1918
War Diary	Sheet 27 Schep.1	17/07/1918	19/07/1918
War Diary	Sheet 28 Scherpenberg.	20/07/1918	31/07/1918
War Diary	Sheet 27 & 28.	31/07/1918	31/07/1918
War Diary	Sheet 27 R.F.A.	01/08/1918	09/08/1918
War Diary	Sheet 28.	08/08/1918	10/08/1918
War Diary	Sheet 27 R.5.a.	10/08/1918	10/08/1918
War Diary	Sheet 27/28 Bn Hqrs at M.17.b.7.5.	10/08/1918	23/08/1918
War Diary		19/08/1918	23/08/1918
War Diary	Sheet 28.	23/08/1918	24/08/1918
War Diary	G.34.b.4.0.	24/08/1918	26/08/1918
War Diary	M.17.b.	26/08/1918	31/08/1918
War Diary	Sheet 28 1/40,000 Kemmel.	01/09/1918	02/09/1918
War Diary	Dickebusch.	02/09/1918	06/09/1918
War Diary	Sheet 28-G.24.	07/09/1918	10/09/1918
War Diary	Dickebusch.	11/09/1918	13/09/1918
War Diary	Sheet 28. Dickebusch	14/09/1918	15/09/1918
War Diary	Licques.	16/09/1918	26/09/1918
War Diary	Licques Brandhoek.	27/09/1918	27/09/1918
War Diary	Brandhoek	28/09/1918	28/09/1918
War Diary	Sheet 28 Brandhoek to Hill 60.	28/09/1918	30/09/1918
War Diary	Sheet 28/P.19 Houthem Area.	01/10/1918	01/10/1918
War Diary	28/J.35.d.	02/10/1918	02/10/1918
War Diary	27/L.	07/10/1918	07/10/1918
War Diary	Dauglas Camp Sheet 28.	08/10/1918	15/10/1918
War Diary	Sheet 29 C/15.	16/10/1918	16/10/1918
War Diary	29/N D.	20/10/1918	26/10/1918
War Diary	Coortrai.	27/10/1918	31/10/1918
War Diary		29/10/1918	30/10/1918
War Diary	Courtrai.	01/11/1918	01/11/1918
War Diary	Sheet 29 P 30 Central and Q19 Central.	02/11/1918	05/11/1918

War Diary	Vichte.	05/11/1918	11/11/1918
War Diary	Sheet 29.		
War Diary	Sheet 30.	12/11/1918	12/11/1918
War Diary	Gemeldorp.	13/11/1918	18/11/1918
War Diary	Waerbeke.	19/11/1918	30/11/1918
War Diary	Tournai 5 Viane.	01/12/1918	11/12/1918
War Diary	Viane/Enghien.	12/12/1918	12/12/1918
War Diary	Enghien Hal	13/12/1918	13/12/1918
War Diary	Sheet Brussells Hal/Waterloo.	14/12/1918	14/12/1918
War Diary	Waterloo.	15/12/1918	15/12/1918
War Diary	Genappe (Loupoigne).	16/12/1918	16/12/1918
War Diary	Loupoigne.	17/12/1918	17/12/1918
War Diary	St. Amand.	18/12/1918	18/12/1918
War Diary	Belgrade.	19/12/1918	19/12/1918
War Diary	Bonnville.	20/12/1918	20/12/1918
War Diary	Wanze.	21/12/1918	31/12/1918
War Diary	(Belgium) Wanze Liege Y C.6.65.45.	01/01/1919	05/01/1919
War Diary	Wanze.	06/01/1919	06/01/1919
War Diary	Germany.	06/01/1919	07/01/1919
War Diary	Hoffnungstnal Z.L. Germany F.2.50.20.	07/01/1919	07/01/1919
War Diary	Germany.	07/01/1919	07/01/1919
War Diary	Lindlar. Sheet 2K. 12.I.18.92.	08/01/1919	19/01/1919
War Diary	Lindlar.	21/01/1919	31/01/1919

WO95/26433(2)

WO95/26433(2)

124th Inf.Bde.
41st Div.

Battn. with Bde. returned to France from Italy 1/6.3.18.

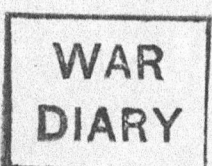

10th BATTN. THE QUEEN'S ROYAL REGIMENT (WEST SURREY).

M A R C H

1 9 1 8

Army Form C. 2118.

WAR DIARY
or
INTELLIGENCE SUMMARY.

10th Bn. Queen's R.W. Surrey Regt.

Place	Date	Hour	Summary of Events and Information	Remarks and references to Appendices
LIMEN?	1st		Bn. Bn. entrained for France in two trains in accordance with orders.	
	5th Mar.		No 85. The journey was much delayed by bad weather. Horses were provided for the men at least twice a day by making use of en-route to en-route to the open trucks. This was unnecessary to latrines was fifteen at suitable time from Haute Epine. The latrine was quick in view.	
Siege of LIGNY	5/6		Bn. Bn. detrained at MONDICOURT and marched to ANT-ST-LEGER where it arrived at billets having until 21st March. The having was in accordance with about frequency. Two days a week was given to special kit to structure while the special squad was immediately engaged in to attach for this was his was continued... at refreshing of the front line. 30% of personnel were found to be specially weak to this B.H.C. 21st to 30th? cases 30% in some battalions found. Practical training gave importance was attached to the use of the rifle. We were of a range every other day which enabled the C.Os. to attach every man in his... to attach every leadership to keeping the men... an efficient as it has been to rapid in action has insufficient work than son...	

G. Strange

Army Form C. 2118.

WAR DIARY
or
INTELLIGENCE SUMMARY.

(Erase heading not required.)

10th B". Queen's R.W. Surrey Regt.

(2)

Place	Date	Hour	Summary of Events and Information	Remarks and references to Appendices
SUS? or LIGER			MARCH	
			As long up to the Forty 9th Day was devoted to trenching and B". Schemes.	
	20.		Orders to the Btn. (9th Queens) from 7th Battalion to take Col. Clark DSO. from 2nd R.W.S. and assumed command of the B". Warning order was received that	
	21.		B" would whom the ACHEUX area. Probably Gilliat at SENLIS trenchline training up to night of 27/28th.	
Asylum			As long as occupied in attached in the operations from March 22nd	
			March:-	
			The B" entrained at SAULTY. News was heard that a large German offensive had begun — that many places many miles back had been shelled. It was soon found that the destination was changed from ALBERT to ACHEUX-LE-GRAND.	
			The B". detrained here at about 1:30 a.m. marched to Camp No. 11 at FARREUIL Sheet 57 c. at H 16.6.	
			* *	Rutherford
BIZRREUIL	30.		The two companies "C" & "D" were to proceed A co. holding front line (Sheet 67D) in position all four platoons in from F.3. to E.3.0. to a point some 200 yds N. of this, the other coys. were hid. a single track; joining the right of the 26th R. Fus. he others to the W.Y.L.I. at E. 2.D.7.2. in support.	

Army Form C. 2118.

WAR DIARY
or
INTELLIGENCE SUMMARY.
(Erase heading not required.)

10th Bn. Queens R.W. Surrey Regt.

(3)

Queen's
R.W. Surrey

Place	Date	Hour	Summary of Events and Information	Remarks and references to Appendices
BUCQUOY	31		MARCH	
			The Batt. Coys were once more placed under the same command. Took over the centre sector of the Bde front. 400 yds in all. 200x N + 200x S of gridline. Relieved F.T. The Coys were disposed A Coy 3 platoons in front line from F28c 3.0. to F28c 5.3½. 1 platoon by in about 100 yds behind the centre of this line. B Coy 2 platoons in front & occupying German trenches dug from L4a 2.10 2 platoons in reserve to the road 200 yds South Bn. HQ. was established at F.27.d.	
			The following statistics cover the period 1/31 March:—	
			Strength at beginning 44 off 858	
			Evacuated sick 93	
			Struck off 10	
			Killed 1 26	
			Wounded 1 145	
			Missing 11 184	
			Reinforcements 4 116	
			28 516	
			Strength at end of month 17 — 274 858	

41st Division.
124th Infantry Brigade

WAR DIARY

10th BATTALION

THE ROYAL WEST SURREY REGIMENT

APRIL 1918

Army Form C. 2118.

WAR DIARY
or
INTELLIGENCE SUMMARY.

10th Queens R. b Surrey

Vol 24

Place	Date	Hour	Summary of Events and Information	Remarks and references to Appendices
BUCQUOY	1/2nd April to 6th		After 10 days fighting in the Battle for Amiens the regiment was relieved and entrained at HALLOY where they rested one day, and after passing in successive days through BONNIERES & FREVENT they entrained to POPERINGHE Fr the STEENVOORD AREA. rested 2 days and marched to BRANDHOEK.	
	7/8th		The Regiment relieved the 2nd Batt. S. Wales Borderers 29 Division, in the PASSCHENDAELE SECTOR holding 1200 yards in 14 Posts S. of the Village B & D Co's in front line A.Co in Support at MOSSELMARK. C.Co in reserve at BELLEWE and until the 14 April the position remained the same; Sector quiet.	
PASSCHENDAELE	13/14th		On this night owing to the success of the enemy S.W. of Ypres it was decided to hold the front line lightly, and withdraw the 26th Division into reserve. The 10th Queens took over then line as well as what they had formerly held, and were responsible for 2200 yards of the front. This was done by thinning the supporting platoons into the line and reducing most posts from two to one section strong. Life was quiet and patrolling was almost impossible owing to the state of the ground.	
	16/April		Owing to the loss of Kemmel Hill it was necessary to withdraw the front	

Army Form C. 2118.

WAR DIARY
or
INTELLIGENCE SUMMARY.
(Erase heading not required.)

Place	Date	Hour	Summary of Events and Information	Remarks and references to Appendices
YPRES	16 April		line near YPRES and at 2 A.m the regiment retired to the defences in front of Ypres. The withdrawal commenced by 3 posts per company moving back, and a similar number every 10 minutes until the whole of the 2 companies less 6 specially selected men per company, had left the line. The ground they had to pass over was so waterlogged and pitted with shell holes that the leading platoon had only marched 1800 yards by 4 A.m. The retirement was covered by the supporting Co at MOSSELMARK who eventually covered the withdrawal of the Regiment. The 6 men per Co left behind to keep up rifle fire and Very lights, retired at 3.30 A.m. and the last act of withdrawal the demolition of BELLEVUE DUGOUTS, WATERLOO & the Bridge on the STEENBECK was completed at 4.30 A.m. The withdrawal was noiseless and undiscovered by the enemy as there was no machine gun fire on the tracks and little shelling the roads. Coys the dying form nil.	
	17 April		The 10 Queens now being at Middlesex Camp outside the Ypres ramparts Commenced the Intermediate zone defences from the SALLY PORT to the	

Army Form C. 2118.

WAR DIARY
or
INTELLIGENCE SUMMARY.
(Erase heading not required.)

Place	Date	Hour	Summary of Events and Information	Remarks and references to Appendices
YPRES	17-30 April		St JEAN Road 1200 yards. This line which ran through the Cemetery has since become the main line of resistance, with an outpost line roughly 1000 yards to the East. Conditions during this period were quiet, with the exception of mustard gas shelling round the areas of the ramparts, 3 & 4 nights in succession. Most of the casualties were caused by men being ordered the trench by working near Shellholes, or by the fumes which were caused strongly when the action of the Sun takes effect. Yes and throughout chiefly affected and generally sickness lasted only three days. Casualties for the 13 days:- 3 Killed. 3 Died of wounds. Wounded. 16 Gassed. On the 18th April the Reg. strength was 5 Officers ORs. 374. Present. Reinforcements during month 20 Officers ORs 577 On 30 April the Reg. strength 38 Officers ORs 1029 on paper.	[signature]

Army Form C. 2118.

WAR DIARY
or
INTELLIGENCE SUMMARY.
(Erase heading not required.)

Instructions regarding War Diaries and Intelligence Summaries are contained in F. S. Regs., Part II. and the Staff Manual respectively. Title pages will be prepared in manuscript.

MAP REF 28 NW 1/20000

Place	Date	Hour	Summary of Events and Information	Remarks and references to Appendices
YPRES	May 6.7.8		Strength at beginning of month. 35 + 1088 O.R. " end of month. 39 - 1113 O.R.	
	night of 2nd/3rd		Batt. still in YPRES defences. Relieved by 18th K.R.R. Batt 122 Inf Bde. Relief complete 12.20 a.m. During this time in the trenches, there was but little activity on the part of the enemy. Artillery fire was normal. On one or two occasions YPRES was shelled with yellow cross gas shells.	
	May / Jun	12.20 a.m	Batt moved to WARRINGTON CAMP H.2.t Div. Reserve. During the day the Batt bathed. BRANDHOEK	
	4th		Commenced work on the YELLOW LINE. Moved from Warrington Camp to O. Camp A.30.D.19.	
	5th to 11th		BRANDHOEK Work on YELLOW LINE. M.C.	
	11th		In the evening the Batt. proceeded to relieve the 16th and part of the 18th Batt of the 6th Div. in the Line and EAST of YPRES.	

M.C. Cartlett
Lt Col.
Cmdg 10th Queens

Army Form C. 2118.

WAR DIARY
or
INTELLIGENCE SUMMARY.
(Erase heading not required.)

Instructions regarding War Diaries and Intelligence Summaries are contained in F. S. Regs., Part II. and the Staff Manual respectively. Title pages will be prepared in manuscript.

Place	Date	Hour	Summary of Events and Information	Remarks and references to Appendices
YPRES.	May 12	3.8 a.m	Relief complete. Hour line. Batt HQrs in RAMPARTS. A Coy in DOLLS A Coy, B Coy, Ramparts. C Coy YPRES defense line. D Coy in Ecole.	
	Night 15/16		A Coy take over Zillebeke Support (I9d + I5b) from 1 Coy of 20th D.L.I.	
	Night 19/20		Relieved the 20th D.L.I. in front line; after being relieved by 26th R.F's Batt HQ at Ecole. Four Coys holding front line from Zillebeke Lake to WHITE CHATEAU.	
	Night 23/24		A Coy (left front line Coy) relieved by 1 Coy of 26th R.Fus and on relief moved to Zillebeke Support line. Batt. HQ moved back to Ramparts. Pte Roughton killed during relief.	
	Night 24/25		1 O.R. W.C.O. + 3 men German Officer captured by B Coy patrol N. of Zillebeke Lake. Relieved by 18 K.R.R & 122 Bde. Moved back to bank of H20. in Div reserve (Green line)	
	27th		Baths. Batt. stood to, owing to enemy attack on Scottish Wood. Situation normal at 3.30 a.m.	

M C Cakcott
Capt. 10th Queen's

Army Form C. 2118.

WAR DIARY
or
INTELLIGENCE SUMMARY.

(Erase heading not required.)

Place	Date	Hour	Summary of Events and Information	Remarks and references to Appendices

	May 28th 29th 30th 31st		Battn. Training Open Warfare. Work on the GREEN LINE.
			
			                         Officers O.R.
			 Casualties Killed 1 Killed 6
			                          W. 1 W. 18
			 Reinforcements 11 167.
			 Strength at end of Month. 39. 1113.
			
			 M.C. Cook Lt Col.
			 Comdg. 10th Queen's.	

WAR DIARY
INTELLIGENCE SUMMARY
(Erase heading not required.)

Army Form C. 2118.

10th Bn "The Queens" R.W. Surrey Regt.

Vol 26

Place	Date	Hour	Summary of Events and Information	Remarks and references to Appendices
YPRES Sheet 28 H 2 a	June 1-2nd		Battn. in Divl Reserve at ORILLIA CAMP. Daily working parties of 8 Off 400 Ranks found for work on GREEN LINE (Elverdinghe-Vlamertinghe)	
—	3rd	9am	Relieved by 1/4th W. Yorks. 146th Inf Bde. Moved by Light Rwy from BARRIE STATION to PUGWASH Sheet 27 E 6 & 8.8. Hence from MENDINGHEM at 3pm to WATTEN arriving there 9pm. Detrained & marched to billets in 2nd Army Training Area W of VOLKERINCKHOVE Transport proceeded to this area by road.	
Hazebrouck 5a 7/40,000 VOLKERINCKHOVE	4-7th		Route marches (Battle order) under Coy arrangements in conjunction with tactical schemes for Lewis Guns.	
—	8th		Battn. marched to AUDREHEM (Sheet Calais 13 1/40,000) via WATTEN - GANSPETTE - BAYENGHEM - NORDAUSQUES - TOURNEHEM - BONNINGUES. Start 3.15 pm. Arrived in billets 12.15 am 9.6.18	
AUDREHEM Sheet Calais 13	10th		Training. Tactical training in open warfare by platoons - Recreational training	
	11th		2 Coys in open warfare. 2 Coys on AUDREHEM 300x range	
	12th		Battn Scheme of training on 'B' Area N of GUEMY.	
	13/14		Baths - remainder of plns spent in open warfare training	
	14/14		Brigade Scheme as per attached.	
	15th		Battalion training on 'B' Area. Instruction in No 36 Mills Grenade	
	17th		Battalion firing on Range. No 5 platoon won Bde final A.R.A Bullet & Bayonet Competition	
	18-19		Bde exercise. Blown rifle machine gun under Coy Arrangements	
	20th		Baths. Lecture on Outposts.	
	21st		Battn. Scheme on 'B' Area.	
	22nd		Inspection by Brig. Gen. J. Alderson C.M.G. DSO. Comdg 124th Infy. Bde. - Training in Outposts under Coy arrgts and lectures on same.	
	24th		2 Coys on Ranges. 2 Coys on 'B' Area training in Outposts	

G. B. Pitt
Lieut Colonel
Comdg 10th Bn "The Queens" R.W.S. Regt.

Army Form C. 2118.

WAR DIARY
or
INTELLIGENCE SUMMARY.
(Erase heading not required.)

Instructions regarding War Diaries and Intelligence Summaries are contained in F. S. Regs., Part II. and the Staff Manual respectively. Title pages will be prepared in manuscript.

Place	Date	Hour	Summary of Events and Information	Remarks and references to Appendices
RUDBROHEN. VOLKERINCHOVE.	25th	8.30am	Battn. marched to VOLKERINCHOVE AREA via BONNINGUES - TOURNEHEM - NORDAUSQUES - BAYENGHEM - GANSPETTE - WATTEN and occupied same billets as vacated on the 8th inst. Arrived in billets 4.30pm. B.D.H.	
"	26th	9.20am	Battn continued march to OUDEZEELE Area via LEDERZEELE - LE TON - WEMAERS CAPPEL L'ANGE - HARDIFORT. Arrived in billets 4.30pm. B.D.H.	
OUDEZEELE	27th 28th 29th		Battalion rested in this Area (Corps Reserve XIV French) B.D.H. B.D.H. B.D.H.	
"	night 30th/1st	6.30pm	Lt. Colonel E. B. NORTH D.S.O Royal Fusiliers took over command of the Battalion. B.D.H. Battalion marched via WINNEZEELE - STEENVOORDE - ABEELE and relieved the 1st Bn. 102nd Regt, of the 4th (French) Division, no variation in nature of the night sub. sector of the XIV French Corps Front. Relief successfully completed by 3.15 a.t, 1st June. B.W.	

Strength beginning of month.   39 Off.   1113 O.Rks.

Reinforcements   3
     22
     6

Casualties -   S.O.R wounded   2
     4
     41

Strength at end of month   40 Off.   1072 O.Rks.

A few cases of influenza occurred during 19th - 24th. One case of scarlet fever. All cases evacuated.

G.B.North.
Lieut. Colonel.
Comdg 10th Bn "The Queens" R.W.S. Regt.

WAR DIARY
or
INTELLIGENCE SUMMARY.

Army Form C. 2118.

(Erase heading not required.)

Place	Date	Hour	Summary of Events and Information	Remarks and references to Appendices
Sheet 24 1/40,000 W. of Reninghelst	30.6.18 1.7.18 2. 3. 4.		The Battn, marching from the OUDEZEELE AREA via WINNEZEELE - STEENVOORDE - ABEELE arrived in the Reserve Area (L·30·c) and relieved the 102nd Regiment (French) Relief complete by 2am. Battn. HQ. located at L·30·c·8·5. 8.R.R. Resting in Reserve Area. Training of Lewis Gunners, instruction in Musketry &c, under Coy Arrangements carried out daily. 8.R.R. Battn. bathed. Commanding Officer attended Brigade conference. Policy of defence, scheme of wiring, supply of ammunition, plans for counter-attack discussed 8.R.R.	
Sheet 28 Scherpenberg	night 5/6th		Battn. moved up and relieved 20th D.L.I in front line. Relief complete by 2am. for disposition of Coys see O.O.101 attached 8.B.) 9.R.R.	
	6 7 8 9		Disposition of Coys unaltered 8.B.) during this period. Enemy infantry inactive. Hostile artillery fairly active, particular attention being paid to S.W. face of SCHERPENBERG. Enemy harrassing fire on tracks and roads nightly. 8.R.R. O/C Commanding Officers attended Bde Commanders conference. Points discussed:- New system of defence, plan of works &c. 8.B.) 9.R.R. Casualties during this tour of duty 10R. 1.OR. killed. 10R. 1.OR. wounded (Capt. Hale "C" Coy killed)	
— " —	night 10/11th 12 13 14		Relieved by 26th R.F and moved back into support. Relief complete 3·15 am 8.R.R Battn. in Support. Working parties found nightly when in the Area.-Digging and R.E. Wiring Reserve Line carrying & burying material &c. to for front line Battn, upkeeping Hut material etc. White flag's with taking 3 days nightly. Enemy infantry inactive. Marked activity of hostile artillery on Scherpenberg and valley M/S·A. 8.R.R. Commanding Officer attended Bde Conference 14th. Points discussed:- Recon of patrols. Provisional Defence Scheme, Wiring accommodation, counter-attack working parties &c. 8.B.)	
Sheet 24 W. of Reninghelst	night 15/16th		Relieved by 26th R.F in support and moved back into Reserve Area (L·30·c). Relief complete 2·50 am. Wdefft ž "C" Coy staying in line for working parties. Heavy shelling of Scherpenberg on 14, 15 H.b.h. 11·45 pm 16th Enemy's peripherious shell carried off by our Artillery. Casualties during this tour of duty:- 2 OR. killed·4 OR· died of Wounds· 9 OR. wounded. 2mm	

WAR DIARY or INTELLIGENCE SUMMARY

Army Form C. 2118.

Place	Date	Hour	Summary of Events and Information	Remarks and references to Appendices
Sheet 24 Scherpl	19/4		Battn in Reserve. Working daily on Westoutre line and burying cable. 3 boys employed one boy resting. Enemy attack expected on night 18/19th. Artillery carried out counter-preparation shoot from 3.45-4.6am. Attack did not develop. Casualties during the tour: 4 wounded.	
		19h.	Commanding Officers attended Bde Conference. Points discussed: 20th Wd. at Duty. Organization, raids, patrols, accommodation, supply of ammunition.	
			Battn relieved 20th. Dt.1 in front line for dispositions of boys see O.O.103 attached.	
Sheet 28 Scherpenberg	night 20/21st		Relief complete by 2am.	
	night 22/23rd		Battn H.Q. moved its position behind Scherpenberg (M18 a 0.8) Rear boy occupying old Battn H.Q. — Battn in front line. Slight decrease in activity of enemy artillery, Scherpenberg still receiving attention, also tracks and roads.	
	23rd		Commanding Officer attended Bde Loutrappe Trench discussed. Training & works.	
	24th		Attachment of Americans. Coy Officers schemes etc. Casualties during this tour of duty: 1 O.R. Killed 5 O.R. Wounded.	
	night 24/25		Relieved in line by 26th. R.F. as per O.O.104 attached and fell back into support Relief complete 12.15am. "C" Coy (110th 1PDOR) 106th. Infty Regt 29th American Division attached to this Unit for tuition in trench warfare. This Coy relieved this "D" Coy in the front line night 28/29th. "D" Coy coming back into support with this Unit.	
			Had British men rendered samples by this attachment (14 Off 1000R) despatched to Westoutre Line (M 8b) which they occupied and worked on.	
	night 24/25th		26th R.F. raided enemy trenches between N19a 95.06 - N19a 85.15. 2 prisoners captured.	
	29th		Enemy infantry inactive during this tour of duty. Enemy artillery still active against the Scherpenberg. There is a notable decrease in hostile shelling. The attack which seemed pending about the 18th. has not materialized. The enemy now showing signs of work on his defensive positions.	
	30th		Casualties: 4 O.Rs. Killed 4 O.R. Wounded.	
	31st 2.20-3.20am		Heavy barrage laid down by enemy on our forward positions. Total Casualties during this tour of duty: 4 O.Rs Killed 4 O.R Wounded.	

Army Form C. 2118.

WAR DIARY
or
INTELLIGENCE SUMMARY.
(Erase heading not required.)

Instructions regarding War Diaries and Intelligence Summaries are contained in F.S. Regs., Part II. and the Staff Manual respectively. Title pages will be prepared in manuscript.

Place	Date	Hour	Summary of Events and Information	Remarks and references to Appendices
Sheet 27425	night 31/10		106th Inty Regt (Americans) relieved 26th R.F. in front line. 26th R.F. relieved 22nd R.F. in support as per O.O. 105 attached. The Battn then moved back to area W of Reninghelst (R5 a.c.). Relief complete 3.20 am. Battn in billets esm. P.B.).	
			Strength at beginning of month.	
			40 Off. 1072 O.Ranks	
Casualties:- Killed			1 Off. 10 "	
Wounded			1 Off. 30 " (20 Off. wounded at duty)	
Reinforcements :-			40 Off. 90 "	
			Strength at end of month	
			38 Off. ✻ 924 OR.	
			✻ This big decrease is due to 113 O.R's being drafted from D.R.C. to Base for transfer to other units.	
			Trench Strength:-	
			(a) Beginning of month 23 Off. 586 O.R.	
			(b) End of month 25 Off. 513 O.R.	
			P.B. Nott	
			Lieut. Colonel.	
			Comdg. 10th (S) Bn "The Queens" R.W. Surrey Regt.	

WAR DIARY
or
INTELLIGENCE SUMMARY
(Erase heading not required.)

Army Form C. 2118.

10th Bn "The Queens" R.W. Surrey Regt.

Place	Date 1918	Hour	Summary of Events and Information	Remarks and references to Appendices
SHEET 24 R.5.a	August 1st		Battalion resting in LOYE AREA. Bn. H.Qrs situated R.5.a.51. Commanding Officer attended Bde. Cmdrs. Conference. Points discussed:- Counter signs. Barrage positions. relief work, zalvage etc.	E.B.N.
	2/4th		Battalion resting, cleaning up. Inspections & training carried out daily under Company arrangements. All companies bathed & clean clothing issued during these dates.	P.B.A.
	5/9th		Training carried out daily as per programme attached.	P.B.A.
	(2 Aug 28) night 8/9th	12 Mn.	3 Offrs & 54 ORanks "B" Coy. under Lieut GIRLING raided enemy trenches between N.24.d.24.36 & N.24.d.50.40. Casualties. 7 ORs. wounded 3 ORanks missing. One N.C.O. 238th R.I.R. 52nd Res. Divn. & one light machine gun captured. In connection with this raid, strong patrols commencing night 3/4th were sent out & the ground thoroughly reconnoitred. Report by OC raid & Operation Order attached.	
	9th		Comdg. Officer attended Bde. Cmdrs. Conference. points discussed:- Attachment of Americans troops. Raids. Work etc.	P.B.A.
	10th		3rd Battn. 108th Inf. Regt. 27th American Division arrived in LOYE AREA at 2/mn. & were amalgamated with this Unit, thus forming 2 Battalions ("C" & "D" Composite)	P.B.A.

Army Form C. 2118.

WAR DIARY
or
INTELLIGENCE SUMMARY.

(Erase heading not required.)

10th Bn "Queens" R.W. Surrey Regt.

Place	Date	Hour	Summary of Events and Information	Remarks and references to Appendices
8/oct 24 R.S.a.	10"		"C" Comp. Bn. Commanded by Major C.E. Edwards MC. (2nd in Cd. this Unit)	
			"D" Comp. Bn. Commanded by Major J. Archelle. D.S.O M.C. (26th R.Suers)	9Bh
			Lt. Col. E.B. North. D.S.O. a/Brigade Commander.	9Bh
Sheet 29/28 Bn HQrs at M.14.G.95.5.	night 10/11"		"C" & "D" Composite Battns. proceeded to the line. "C" relieved 1st Bn. 108th Inf. Regt.	9Bh
	11/12"		in front line. - "D" relieved 20th D.L.1 in Support. Operation Order for more attached	
			Battalion in line. Enemy attitude quiet but nervous. Counter preparation	
			shoots carried out by our Artillery daily between 3 am & 11 am. Enemy	9Bh
- " -	night 12/13"		retaliation fairly heavy on our forward system	9Bh
	14/15"		Half "D" Bn. relieved half "C" in front line. Relief complete. 2:30 am.	9Bh
			Remainder of "D" Bn. relieved "C" in front line. Relief complete 3 am.	9Bh
			Heavy shelling of SCHERPENBERG between 10-11 p.m. Casualties during this tour	
	16/17"		of duty. 1 Off. & 5 O.r. Killed. 20 o.rs Wounded. 3 o.rs. missing	
	18/19"		108th Inf. Regt. took over the duties of the front line. This unit moving to Support.	9Bh
			Relief complete. 1:35 am. 108th Inf. Regt. relieved by 26th R.F. in the front line	9Bh
	19/20		This unit remaining in Support.	9Bh
	19/23		Battalion in Support. Comdg. Officer attended Bde. Comdrs. Conference	9Bh

Army Form C. 2118.

WAR DIARY
or
INTELLIGENCE SUMMARY.
(Erase heading not required.)

10th Bn "Queens" R.W. Surrey Regt

Place	Date	Hour	Summary of Events and Information	Remarks and references to Appendices
SUFFOLK	night 23/24		Battalion relieved by 26th R.F. & moved into Reserve. Batn. HQrs situated at BRASSERIE RENINGHELST. Relief complete 12.30 a.m.	9.B.h.
G.H.Q.2	24/26		Battalion in Reserve Area. Platoon training & range practice carried out. All companies bathed.	9.B.h.
M.17.b	night 26/27		Battalion relieved 26th R.F. in Support. Relief complete 1.30 a.m.	9.B.h.
	27/29		Batn. in Support	9.B.h.
	night 29/30		Battalion relieved 20th D.L.I. in the Right Sub Sector (front line) Relief complete 2.0 a.m.	9.B.h.
	30th		Battalion in line. Information received of enemy withdrawal on right. Strong patrols sent out discovered the enemy had evacuated. Patrols were pushed forward which met with no resistance. These were beyond KENNEL HILL on early morning 31st. Bn HQrs established at MARJORIE POST. A minor operation to straighten line carried out, forward HQrs situated at DONEGAL FARM. On completion of the move line ran just N of the knoll line running S from LINDENHOEK. (SHERPENTIER SWITCH)	9.B.h. 9.B.h. R.W.S.
			Batn. was relieved in front line by 14th Cheshire Regt. (34th Div) & moved to Suffolk on 2.00.p.m. front N of the railway	
No SCHERPENBERG AREA	night 31st		Batn. was to have entrained for TILQUES AREA on relief but owing to operations this move was not carried out.	9.B.h.

Army Form C. 2118.

WAR DIARY
or
INTELLIGENCE SUMMARY.
(Erase heading not required.)

10th Queen's R.W.S. Regt.

Place	Date	Hour	Summary of Events and Information	Remarks and references to Appendices
			In connection with the raid on 8/9", the following awards were granted. Lieut. J.E.B. Guling - M.C. Military Medal to 9448 Sergt. KING.F.J 256444 Sergt. SMITH.S 59924 Pte PAYNE A. 242454 L/Cpl RINGROSE W.T. 25410 Pte W. JAMES 259144 Pte ASHTON J. (P²⁵ᵃˡᵗᵉ) 242066 Sergt KILLICK was also awarded M.M for carrying dispatches under a heavy barrage. STRENGTH beginning of month. 38 officers. 924 O.Rs. TOTAL CASUALTIES. Killed. 1 Officer 8 O.Rs. Wounded 39 O.Rs. Missing 3 O.Rs. REINFORCEMENTS 7 officers 103 O.Rs STRENGTH end of month. 41 officers 914 O.Rs.	9 B h
	7.9.18.		J.B. North Lieut-Colonel. Commanding 10th Bn. "Queens" R.W.S. Regt.	

Army Form C. 2118.

1924
4
10th Queens R.W.S. Regt.
9629

WAR DIARY
or
INTELLIGENCE SUMMARY.
(Erase heading not required.)

Instructions regarding War Diaries and Intelligence Summaries are contained in F. S. Regs., Part II. and the Staff Manual respectively. Title pages will be prepared in manuscript.

Place	Date	Hour	Summary of Events and Information	Remarks and references to Appendices
Sheet 28 H0.000 KEMMEL	1/2nd Sept.		Battn in Front Line. Relieved by 4th Bn Michigan Regt 102nd Infy Bde and fell back into Reserve Area (OUDERDOM) Battn HO situated 9.2H 6.68	93.h
DICKEBUSCH	2/3rd		Battn relieved 2nd Bn 105th Infy Regt 27th American Division in Front Line (DICKEBUSCH SECTOR) Dispositions as pers O.O.121 attached	93.h
"	3rd		Battn in Line. Dispositions unaltered	
"	4th?		Battn attached enemy at 5.30 am. Report on operations attached	
"			Casualties suffered by Battn in this attack were 10ff 120R Killed 2 offs 240 ORks wounded 93.h. Battn relieved by 2 bys of 10th R.W. Kents and 2 bys of 24th Royal Fusiliers in the front line and fell back into Reserve at OUDERDOM. Occupied same billets as on night 2/2nd inst.	93.h
Sheet 28 - 9.24	7-10th		Battn in Reserve. 1st day devoted to cleaning up and re-equipment. Battn Bestial Training carried out - musketry - platoon drills and specialist training. Casualties whilst in Reserve:- 10ORks killed 1ORank wounded	93.h
Dickebusch	11/12th		Battn relieved 26th Royal Fusiliers in outpost and come under command of 123rd Infy Bde. Dispositions as pers O.O. 124 attached. Casualties during this tour of duty - 2 ORanks wounded.	93.h
	13th			

Army Form C. 2118.

WAR DIARY
or
INTELLIGENCE SUMMARY.
(Erase heading not required.)

Instructions regarding War Diaries and Intelligence Summaries are contained in F. S. Regs., Part II, and the Staff Manual respectively. Title pages will be prepared in manuscript. Page 2.

Place	Date	Hour	Summary of Events and Information	Remarks and references to Appendices
Sheet 28 Rickelwich	night 14/15th		Relieved in Support by 10th R.W. West Kents and moved back to Eirton Lines	9.B.h.
		9.22h 5th	when Batt'n embussed and proceeded to LICQUES Pas-de-Calais	
			Arrived there 11 am 15th. Orders for move attached.	9.B.h.
LICQUES	16/26th		Battalion in training – General Policy as follows:-	
			(a) Platoon, Company and Battalion Drill	
			(b) Gas drill, Musketry and frequent lectures	
			(c) Infiltration schemes "Peaceful penetration"	
			(d) Attack on a strong point with Machine Guns	
			(e) Attack and defence generally	
			(f) Moving to and getting on a forming up line by night and day	9.B.h.
			(g) Night operations	
Licques / Brandhoek	27th		Batt'n moved forward to Brandhoek (sheet 28) – 2 Coys by train and 2 Coys by Buses. Accommodated for the night in H4 of a.c. Operation orders for move attached.	9.B.h.
Brandhoek	28th	9am	Battalion moved up the line for attack on the enemy. Operation orders for attack are attached.	9.B.h.

10th Queens. R.W.S. Regt Oct 18

174/41

Army Form C. 2118.

WAR DIARY
or
INTELLIGENCE SUMMARY
(Erase heading not required.)

26

Place	Date	Hour	Summary of Events and Information	Remarks and references to Appendices
Sheet 28 Brandhoek to Hill 60	28/9/18		Battalion marched from BRANDHOEK to HILL 60 where they assembled in Battle formation and prepared to attack the enemy	A1
	29-30th		Battalion attacking. Gained all objectives (line of River Lys between GUNINES and WERVICQ) and consolidated in depth.	A1
Sheet 28 N.19 Houthem Corner	Oct 1st		Battalion was relieved by 23rd London Regt and moved into billets for the night along the Canal Bank between HOLLEBEKE and HOUTHEM BRIDGE	A1
28/J356d	2nd		Battalion marched to KRUISEECK area where it remained in Brigade Reserve until 6th October	A1
	4th		Battalion marched to BIRR CROSS ROADS and entrained for ABEELE at 0900 8th October	A1
Douglas Camp	8/12th		Assisting an Douglas Camp resting and reorganising	A1
Sheet 28	13th		Battalion marched out to take part in the MENIN Battle. Entrained at REMY SIDING (J.23 4.9.) detrained at CLAPHAM JUNCTION (J.13.a.)	A1
	14th		Battalion marched to Assembly Area and prepared to attack Jno. NM 0530	A1
	15th		Objectives were gained & the Battn. were relieved by 24th Queens. Billeted for the night in the vicinity of JOHNSTON FARM (28 M 36)	A1

174/41

Army Form C. 2118.

WAR DIARY
or
INTELLIGENCE SUMMARY.
(Erase heading not required.)

Place	Date	Hour	Summary of Events and Information	Remarks and references to Appendices
Sheet 29 8/15	16th		Marched from there to GULLEGHEM and there rested until 19th Oct.	85
21/N 2	20th		Marched to T'HOOGHE Area. Reached with 700.	85
	26th		Battalion attacking Objective — Line of River SCHELDT E. of COURTRAI and were in action continuously until 26th October when Batn was relieved by 17th & 18th Bn Lancashire Fusiliers and passed through to rest Billets in KOURTRAI	85
COURTRAI	24/31st		Battalion resting and reorganising in Courtrai.	85
			A complete report on all actions is attached giving casualties, captures etc.	85
			Strength at beginning of month 39 Off. 845 O.Ranks Casualties 2 Off 24 O.Rks Wounded 10 Off 142 O.Ranks Missing 04 10 Ranks Reinforcements 4 Off 42 O.Ranks Strength at end of month 31 Off 647 O.Ranks Evacuations 114 O.Ranks	

Browne Major
Comdg 10th Bn "The Queens" R.W.S. Regt

WAR DIARY
or
INTELLIGENCE SUMMARY.
(Erase heading not required.)

Army Form C. 2118.

Place	Date	Hour	Summary of Events and Information	Remarks and references to Appendices
	29/30		Battalion in Action, report of which will accompany next months War Diary	
			Officers O.Ranks	
			Strength at beginning of Month. 38 856	
			Reinforcements 5 94	
			Evacuations 1 50	
			Killed 1 23	
			Wounded 2 73	
			Strength at end of month 39 804	
			P. B. Nott Lt Colonel Comdg 10th (S) Bn. "The Queens" Regt.	

Army Form C. 2118.

WAR DIARY
or
INTELLIGENCE SUMMARY.
(Erase heading not required.)

10th (S) Bn. "The Queens" R.W.S. Regt.

Place	Date	Hour	Summary of Events and Information	Remarks and references to Appendices
COURTRAI	Nov 1st		Battn resting in COURTRAI since 27th ult. Proceeded to relieve the 10th D.L.I on the line marching via SNEVEGHEM — LOCT 6 to KROTE area resting here for tea continued march to the line at 1800 hours. Relief complete 2330 hours. Battn H.Q. situated at 29/P18.c.2.3. Disposition of Coys as per Operations orders attached. Battn on the line. Enemy infantry and artillery inactive during the hour.	98h
Shut 29				98r
P30 b2/6th ult 2nd				96h
6/9 last night 4th			Retired by 15th N.Z.L.I and 15th Sherwoods. Fell back into Queens billets at VICHTE. Relief complete and Battn settled in billets by 0100 hours 5th. Casualties during this tour of duty 1OR Killed 2 OR wounded	
VICHTE	5th/9th		Resting in VICHTE area. Training for assault on River Scheldt. Information received that enemy were retiring from the Scheldt. Battn moved forward to CASTER making the following arrangements, arriving the Scheldt marching via Q21.c.2.9 — BRUGGE Q23.a.H.O —OWAELDESTRAAT— R19.b.6.1 — R20.d.3.5 — R.25.a.5.1 — R.22.a.2.7 — R.16.b.7.1. R.23.b.6.9 — M.20.a.9.5 — M.20.b.1.2 passed through the Scheldt Lyffs Q21 and finally ended in the SCROOKISSE Road arriving there at 4pm.	97h
	10th			98h
	11th		Continued the advance via OPBRAGEL — A22 central N.14.a.7.2. N.21.d.2.8	98h

Army Form C. 2118.

WAR DIARY
or
INTELLIGENCE SUMMARY.
(Erase heading not required.)

Instructions regarding War Diaries and Intelligence Summaries are contained in F. S. Regs., Part II. and the Staff Manual respectively. Title pages will be prepared in manuscript.

Place	Date	Hour	Summary of Events and Information	Remarks and references to Appendices
Shut 29			6.90.c.9.6 - 02b.7.8 - 02y.a.2.4 - 10.28.8.8 - 023.c.8.2 - 024.c.8.6 - Pigeon	
			Notification received the Counter Attack was anticipated and consequently front line	
			was Hostilities issued from Battn Batta's formally relieved at TERBEEK	P.B.U.
			1st NEDERBRAKEL	
Shut 30	12th	9am	Battn marched to GENELDORP arriving here at 11.30am	9.8.4
GENELDORP	13th/14th		Resting and cleaning up.	
	15th		The Division being one of the 8 British Divisions detailed for reorganisation of German territory under the terms of the Armistice continued the advance the	
			Battn marching to WAERBEKE via P26.a.3.8 - P.14.a.7.5 - IDEGHEM - SANTE BERGHEM	9.B.4
			NEUWENHOVE arriving in Billets Billeting parties being sent on ahead	9.B.4
WAERBEKE	19th		Resting	9.B.4
	20th		Marched to VANE via GRIMMERGHES - MOREBEKE Battn in Billets by 4pm	9.B.4
	21/30th		Stationed at VANE. Light training carried out.	
			Strength of Battn beginning of month 34 Off 649 ORks	
			Reinforcements 5 Off 93 ORks	
			Evacuated wounded 4 ORks	
			Evacuated sick 3 Off 84 ORks	
			Strength at end of month 380ff 645 ORks	

E. B. North Lt. Col.
Comdg 10R (S) Bn the Queens R W S Regt

Army Form C. 2118.

WAR DIARY
or
INTELLIGENCE SUMMARY.
(Erase heading not required.) 10th (S) Bn "The Queens" R.W.Surr. Regt.

Instructions regarding War Diaries and Intelligence Summaries are contained in F. S. Regs., Part II. and the Staff Manual respectively. Title pages will be prepared in manuscript. DECEMBER

Place	Date	Hour	Summary of Events and Information	Remarks and references to Appendices
TOURNAI / VIANE	1st		Ceremonial Church Parade. Afternoon devoted to Football & recreation	
	2nd		Battalion carrying out light training. Morning Route march VIANE - BOSCH STRAAT	
	3/4th		BIEVENE - BASSILLY and return	
	5th		Coys under R.S.M. for Coy Drill - N.C.O's under A.G.S Instructors	
			Battalion Parade - 12.00 noon	
	6th		N.R. Coys route marching. GRAMMONT & return, C & D Coys bathing	
			C & D Coys route marching. GRAMMONT & return A & B Coys bathing	
	7th		Battalion route march - BIEVENE & return	
	8th		Ceremonial Church Parade. All afternoon being devoted to recreation	
	9th		Company Drill 9 - 11.30 a.m. Battalion parade 12.00 a.m.	
	10th		Battalion route march VIANE - HERMONT - MILE 13 and return	
	11th		Regimental Commander presented French Decorations in GRAMMONT SQUARE	
VIANE	12th		The Battn representing 17th & Infy Bde	
ENGHIEN			Division commenced forward march to GERMANY; This Battn marching out of billets at 07.30 hours via HERMONT - ENGHIEN	Attached here Maps.
ENGHIEN	13th		Continued the march to dal arrived in billets 2 p.m.	
	14th			

Army Form C. 2118.

WAR DIARY
or
INTELLIGENCE SUMMARY.
(Erase heading not required.)

Instructions regarding War Diaries and Intelligence Summaries are contained in F.S. Regs., Part II. and the Staff Manual respectively. Title pages will be prepared in manuscript.

Place	Date	Hour	Summary of Events and Information	Remarks and references to Appendices
Sheet BRUSSELS				
HAL				
WATERLOO	14th		March continued via BOYSINGHEM - X Rds too yds SE of BUYSINGHEM STN.	
			to WATERLOO. Arrived in billets 2 pm.	Attached Lieut Wayn
WATERLOO	15th		Resting	
GENAPPE (LOUPOIGNE)	16th		March continued via MT ST JEAN to GENAPPE. Marched past HM the	
			King of the Belgians at 13 hrs. (x Rds at Kilo 26). Arrived in billets - LOUPOIGNE - at 1.30pm	
LOUPOIGNE	17th		March continued via Kilo 30 - QUATRE-BRAS - SOMBREFFE 18 to ST AMAND	
			Arrived in billets 2.30 pm.	
ST AMAND	18th		March continued via LIGNY - BOIGNES - ST MARTIN - ONOZ - SPY STN - TEMPLOUX	
			Arrived in billets 3.30 pm. Distance 21 kilos	
BELGRADE	19th		March continued via NAMUR via the South bank of the River Meuse to BONNVILLE	
			passed starting point 12.15. Arrived in billets 14.30 hours	
BONNVILLE	20th		March continued via SCAYEN South bank of the Meuse to HUY	
			Halts arriving at WANZE arriving at 14.30 hours.	
WANZE	21st		Finally resting and cleaning up	
" "	22/		Baths, leathers and boots at Company commanders disposal for light	
	26		training kit, clothing & boot inspections Education classes	

Army Form C. 2118.

WAR DIARY
or
INTELLIGENCE SUMMARY.
(Erase heading not required.)

Instructions regarding War Diaries and Intelligence Summaries are contained in F. S. Regs., Part II. and the Staff Manual respectively. Title pages will be prepared in manuscript.

Place	Date	Hour	Summary of Events and Information	Remarks and references to Appendices
WANZE				
	27th		Assembled daily from 09.00 to 11.00 hours. Afternoons being devoted to recreation. Regular programmes being drawn up for coming training and platoon football competitions	About
	28/31st		Battalion Xmas Dinner. Platoon training carried out. Afternoons devoted to recreation	
			Officers O.R's	
			Strength at beginning of month 38 645	
			Reinforcements 2 244	
			Evacuations 1 72	
			Demobilised - 12	
			Strength at end of month 39 800	

Hingley Dill.
Major
Comdg 13th The Queen's R. W. Regt.

WAR DIARY
INTELLIGENCE SUMMARY

10th Bn. "The Queens" R.W. Surrey Regt.

Army Form C. 2118.

Jan '19

No 33

Place	Date	Hour	Summary of Events and Information	Remarks and references to Appendices
(BELGIUM) WANDRE Lat 50°38' E.Long 5°40'	1919 1/Jan/19		Battalion stationed at WANDRE. Platoon training carried out. Education (Group A. yet) classes in all Companies in morning. Voluntary classes in French Shorthand & Book Keeping in evenings. Baths or attempt at Baths. HOY. Sports in afternoons - Football, Running & Boxing. Officers Riding School at 2pm daily.	^
	Jan 4/19		Battalion Concert Party ("SPARE PARTS") gave an entirely new show in the "Queens" Hall at 18:00hr.	^
	5		Divine Service for all denominations.	^
	6		Classes & Concert Party in the "Queens Hall"	^
WANDRE	6/1/19		Battalion moved out of GERMANY as per Order No. 24 attacked. The left of the whole at 10.00 hr for HOY STATION. Entrained at H.Q.B.N. Motor Lorries were arranged for the men en route.	^
GERMANY HOFFNUNGSTHAL Lat 50° 57' N. Long 7° 20'00	7/1/19		Battalion detrained at HOFFNUNGSTHAL at 06.00. Breakfast was provided. Battalion moved off at 08.30 hr for LINDLAR.	^
			Halted at 12.00 hrs for dinner near OVERATH.	^

Army Form C. 2118.

WAR DIARY
or
INTELLIGENCE SUMMARY.
(Erase heading not required.)

10th Bn "Queens" R.W.S. Regt.

Instructions regarding War Diaries and Intelligence Summaries are contained in F. S. Regs., Part II. and the Staff Manual respectively. Title pages will be prepared in manuscript.

Place	Date	Hour	Summary of Events and Information	Remarks and references to Appendices
GERMANY	7/12		Halted for tea at 16.00 hrs. near ERNSTSHOVEN.	
			ENGELSKIRCHEN to LINDLAR arriving in Billets at 18.45.	
			Met by Guides for men on arrival.	
LINDLAR Sheet 2.K. 12.I. 18.92	8/12		C. & D. Coys. marched off at 10.00 hrs. to take over Outpost line as per order no. 25 attached. Posts taken over from 16th Canad. Battn.	
			at M.T. 82.15 – 11.S.14.31 – 11.T.18.44 – 11.Y.04.3 – 11.T.50.04 & 11.I.30.50	
			Coy "B" at FREILINGSDORF & KAPPELKEN.	
			Bn. HQ. & two companies remained at LINDLAR.	
	8/12		Companies in LINDLAR carried out Coy training. Group "A" Subjects in the School. Football etc. in afternoons.	
	12"		Divine Service.	
	12/14"		General Training carried out in mornings & recreation in afternoon.	
			Company lecture dances, whist drives etc. in the Concert Hall.	
	18"		Bath at ENGELSKIRCHEN.	
	19"		Lecture on road to COLOGNE.	
			Divine Services.	

Army Form C. 2118.

WAR DIARY
or
INTELLIGENCE SUMMARY.
(Erase heading not required.)

10th Bn "Queens" R.W.S. Regt.

Place	Date	Hour	Summary of Events and Information	Remarks and references to Appendices
LINDAR	21st	2.30	Company relieved at Outpost line carried out. Outer arrant	
		3.30	Y.C.T. range booked. Company training. Football in afternoon.	
			Relocation. Evening classes in German trench & shorthand commenced 2.30	
	26/8		Concerts a Dance - Cinema Halls in evenings	
			C. relieved A. in Outpost line. A Coy. training for Int. Company	
			Construction. B. Coy. - General training.	

Strength at beginning of month.   Offrs.   OR.
                                       34   795

Evacuations   1   24
Remobilised   -   43
Struck off for other causes.   1   3
                                       2   70
                                       2   70
                                      35   725
Reinforcements   -   19
                                      35   744
Strength at end of month.

A Hughes? Lt Major
Comdg: 10th Bn "Queens" R.W.S. Regt

www.ingramcontent.com/pod-product-compliance
Lightning Source LLC
Chambersburg PA
CBHW081248170426
43191CB00037B/2086